Scientific Vortex Information

An M.I.T.-Trained
Scientist's
Program

by

PETE A. SANDERS JR.

The Free Soul Method

How to Easily Understand,
Find, and Tap Vortex Energy
in Sedona and Wherever You Travel!

Free Soul Publishing
P.O. Box
Sedona, AZ

Illustrations by Pete A. Sanders Jr.

Sedona Pictures by John Faulconer of Norfolk, VA

(except those of Chapel of the Holy Cross)

Thanks to Lori Levin of Sedona, AZ

for Photos of the Chapel of the Holy Cross

Sedona Vortex Map courtesy of
Light Technology, Flagstaff, Arizona

ISBN 0-9641911-5-6
Published by Free Soul, Sedona, Arizona (1st in 1992)

Printed in the United States by
GraphTech, Flagstaff, Arizona

This booklet is published and distributed by Free Soul, P.O. Box 1762, Sedona, AZ 86339, with the written permission of the author, Pete A. Sanders Jr. Use of the title "Scientific Vortex Information" is also authorized by the author, Pete A. Sanders Jr.

10 9 8 7 6

This Booklet is dedicated to

the unlimited potential

of all Free Souls

everywhere!

Contents

* * *

* * *

* * *

* * *

About the Author

Pete A. Sanders Jr. is an honors graduate of Massachusetts Institute of Technology, where he majored in Bio-Medical Chemistry with a minor in Brain Science. Accepted to attend Harvard Medical School, he chose instead to pursue independent research into the limitlessness of the human mental, physical, and spiritual potential. In 1980, after traveling the world for five years field-testing and polishing the breakthrough techniques he discovered at M.I.T., he settled in Sedona and founded Free Soul, a NonProfit Mind/Body Education Program. Free Soul is a fully federally certified Tax-Exempt Public Education Program designed to help people learn to be *their own* teachers in pioneering their mental and spiritual frontiers. Pete Sanders is the author of the New Age bestseller *You Are Psychic!*, as well as *Access Your Brain's Joy Center* and *The Dynamics of Being a Free Soul* Comprehensive Course. In 1982, in response to student requests, he developed a unique approach for understanding vortexes and easily tapping their energy. If you would like further information about Free Soul or Mr. Sanders' latest developments, check our web site at http://freesoul.net on the internet or write to Free Soul, P.O. Box 1762, Sedona, AZ 86339.

History of the Free Soul Vortex Approach

Founded in Sedona in 1980, Free Soul began its semi-annual national retreats here in 1981. Free Soul instructors and graduates came from around the country for advanced training in the beauty of Sedona. Upon hearing about the vortexes, many were confused by what they felt were overly mystical explanations. Frequently students said, "Pete, we really enjoy your scientific approach to the psychic senses and to the extra dimensions of consciousness that are the Soul. Is there anything practical you can teach about the vortexes? Everything I read seems too mumbo-jumboish. Isn't there a simpler, more understandable approach?" Because of those requests Free Soul started offering semiannual vortex retreats in 1982. This booklet and/or cassette tape are a condensed version of our "Creating Your Own Enlightenment" Comprehensive 4-Day Vortex Retreat. In it we share an approach to the vortexes that makes it possible for you to enhance and turbo-boost *any* spiritual skill that you can conceive. Our purpose is to help you learn how to be your own teacher for the rest of your life. We're not interested in just taking you someplace and "wowing" you. We want to help you learn how to make *every day* a vortex retreat.

There are many incredibly beautiful and powerful spiritual sites in the Sedona area. I feel, however, that someone who is merely having a phenomenal experience without knowing how the effect was created, receives only a small fraction of the benefit possible. They may have the blessing of a beautiful memory or meditation, but they won't be able to repeat the experience when they later want to or need to. The ultimate breakthrough is being able to understand how the vortexes turbo-boost you and how *you* can extend that process for the rest of your life.

The Spiritual Heritage of Sedona

Vortex is just the latest label that has been used to describe Sedona's energy centers, in the same way "channelers" and "channeling" is nothing more than the latest terminology for the ability to trance. Back in the 1960s when I first visited Sedona there were no vortexes, just as in the fifties and sixties when I was first learning, searching and training there were no channelers. Back then channelers were called mediums. In ancient Greece they were called oracles, soothsayers, prophets, and seers. The spiritual skill was the same, the label has just changed. The same type of terminology shift is true of vortexes.

Sedona has been known for its powerful meditation sites for fifty years or as long as five thousand years (depending on whom you listen to). Reflecting the recent heritage, Lois Kellogg, one of the Kellogg cereal company's heiresses, founded a spiritual meeting center near Red Rock Crossing in the 1950s. The center provided a location for meditation, discussion, and the exploration of spirituality. After her death the land was eventually sold to the Forest Service and now adds to the public recreation area at Red Rock Crossing.

Sedona's spiritual heritage extends far earlier, however. Many archeologists believe that thousands of years ago the Native American tribes that inhabited this part of Northern Arizona held the Sedona-Oak Creek Canyon area as a sacred site because ruins of their habitations ring the area. They believe that the Anasazi ("the ancient ones") lived outside of Sedona and visited the Red Rock area only for sacred purposes (ceremonies on the mesa tops or in the creek). In fact, to this day some of the Yavapai Apache Indians make a yearly trip to Oak Creek for a cleansing bath that is similar in style to the yearly pilgrimage to the Ganges made by devoted Hindus.

Origin of the Term "Vortex"

While there are still conflicting reports about who used the term "vortex" first, it appears that the term was coined to describe Sedona's traditional meditation sites in November, 1980 by a channeler named Page Bryant. Page Bryant is a trance medium who travels and lectures nationally. For many years she lived in Sedona, and in one of her weekly channeling sessions she referred to four of the known meditation sites as "the vortexes." Since that time those four areas—Bell Rock, Airport Mesa, Cathedral Rock, and Boynton Canyon—became known as Sedona's primary vortex locations. That term and the promotion of these areas as "The Vortexes" was popularized and further spread nationally by Dick Sutphen in his seminars, books, and tapes. Free Soul's approach to vortexes is a more expansive view. We

11

consider these four areas just a fraction of the energy sources and sites that you can tap in Sedona. We also show you how to find vortexes worldwide. This booklet will give you information on Sedona's eight most powerful areas that are easily accessible. You will also learn a system for finding vortex energy wherever you travel for the rest of your life.

What Is a Vortex?

Free Soul uses a system of explaining vortexes that is not written or described anywhere else. Not only is our approach unique, but I think you will find it much easier to understand as well as more practical to apply. Most writings about the vortexes describe them as electric, magnetic, or electromagnetic sites. This is the terminology used by Page Bryant in her original channeling and also by Dick Sutphen. There are two problems with this labeling system. First of all, it is technically inaccurate.

As a scientist, I can tell you that you can take whatever measuring equipment you want, no matter how sensitive, out to these vortex sites and you will not be able to measure any significant electric or magnetic field difference at the sites. That is why the skeptics attack the idea of the vortexes and people who believe in them. They say, "They're all a bunch of quacks! There is no difference in the magnetic field at the sites." Once as I gave a radio interview in Sedona answering questions about the vortexes, one caller responded, "Vortexes, smortexes! My dictionary says a vortex is a whirlpool of water, like going down a toilet, and that's what I think about all this!"

The term "vortex" is more symbolic than literal. Most vortex energy sites *do not* have a circular energy flow. Rather, they are areas of enhanced linear energy flow. That energy is neither electric nor magnetic. What's happening in the vortexes are energy flows that exist in dimensions deeper than electricity and magnetism. This may sound mystical, but actually it's based on the latest in science.

The Breakthrough of "Superstrings"

The biggest breakthrough in physics in the second half of the twentieth century started sweeping the planet in 1985. Physics is literally seeing a revolution of the size and scope created by Einstein's discoveries of the 1920s and 1930s. This new field of physics in laymen's terms is called "string" theory, or "superstrings." It can be described simply as follows: Subatomic physicists are always trying to find the smallest bit of "stuff" that makes up all things. They feel they've identified it, and they call that smallest bit, *a string*. They picked a common name like string instead of quark or neutrino or pi meson because these strings literally tie together all the forces, energies, and theories of the universe. If you twist them one way, these strings will become a proton; twist them another way and they become an electron; twist them still a different way and they become a photon of light; twist them still another way and they become a graviton, the mysterious particle or force that makes gravity work.

13

That's the boring physics lecture part. The fascinating spiritual part is that the top physicists around the world—M.I.T., Princeton, Cal-Tech, Berkeley, Oxford, Germany, Russia—all agree that these strings exist in a minimum of *ten or more* dimensions. Three of space, one of time, and then they say very rapidly, "and-six-other dimensions-we-don't-have-the-technology-to-measure-into-yet." For the first time the top scientists around the world are admitting that there are dimensions *beyond* that we don't have a clue how to measure technologically. Even though we cannot build machines to measure into those dimensions yet, you can still experience them *because you exist in them*. If the strings exist in ten dimensions, then this page you are reading exists in ten dimensions, you exist in ten dimensions, and so do the vortex sites. What is happening at the vortex sites is energy flow in those deeper dimensions. You have the inner ability to measure, feel, find, and tap that energy. In fact, you have already experienced vortex energy but probably just weren't aware of it.

How to Understand & Label Vortexes—Simply

In Free Soul we use a labeling system that helps you understand what's going on at the site and how to tap it rather than merely make a mystery of it. We label vortexes based on *the direction of energy flow* at the site. Most vortexes have one of two dominant patterns: Upflow vortexes are locations where the energy is flowing upward out of the earth:

14

inflow vortexes are locations where energy is flowing inward into the planet (see Figure 1).

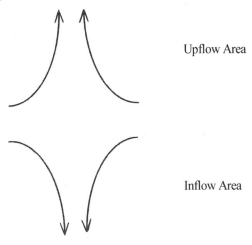

Upflow Area

Inflow Area

Figure 1. Inflow and upflow pattern description

This pattern is repeated throughout nature. An electrical pulse moves along a nerve axon because of an inflow and outflow of ions across the nerve membrane. The cycle of water also mirrors this pattern (upflow as evaporation, downflow as rain). Even the earth's crust does this. There are locations a round the Earth where new crust is flowing up and outward. The largest is called the mid-Atlantic ridge, halfway between the United States and France. There, at the bottom of the ocean, new crust is constantly rising up and spreading out. Thus each year Europe and the U.S. are moving a little farther apart. At sites such as the Marianas Trench off Japan, the deep ocean trenches off Chile, and the subduction zone off the coast of the U.S. Pacific Northwest—these are places where the earth's crust is plunging

15

into the mantle. The Earth's crust is actually recycling, but on a macroscopic time scale. (Isn't it satisfying to know Mother Earth recycles?) It makes sense that the same pattern would repeat on deeper dimensional levels.

As yet, science can't totally explain technologically why the vortex energy patterns exist. It is reasonable, however, to think of it as biospheric energy balancing on those deeper dimensions (the same way there are balancing cycles in the three-dimensional energy flows of atmospheric wind patterns and ocean currents). What is important at this point is for you to learn how you can ride these deeper dimensional energy flows. Then you can tap the vortexes to turbo-boost the host of enhanced mental and spiritual skills that await your exploration. Just as hawks and eagles soar on thermal wind currents, Upflow Vortexes help your Soul reach greater heights of awareness. Inflow Vortexes help you go inward more easily.

Remember that human pioneering has always preceded technology. Columbus wasn't able to say, "Hey, Marco, bring me that satellite photo; let's see where we're going." Daniel Boone, Kit Carson, and Lewis and Clark couldn't call AAA for a triptik. Human exploration has always preceded technology. You can sit back and wait a hundred years for some lab scientist to say, "We now have the technology to measure vortex energy. You have permission to go." Or you can start exploring *now* for yourself. Further, once you think in terms of the flow at the site, it becomes easy to understand what spiritual skills will be turbo-boosted there.

What Skills Vortexes Turbo-Boost

The second problem with the electric/magnetic labeling system and the other two common labeling systems (masculine/feminine and positive/negative) is that the labels alone don't give you a clue about what meditations the sites can assist. (So something's an electric vortex; what are you supposed to do, go there and make like a light bulb? Are only women allowed in a feminine vortex?) When the labeling system doesn't help you understand what to do at the vortex, the site (rather than what the human spirit can do) becomes phenomenalized. People consequently become devoted to a site rather than cherishing their own unlimited potentials. Free Soul's upflow/inflow labeling system makes it easy to figure out what spiritual skills will be assisted by what vortexes.

Upflow Energy

Upflow vortexes turbo-boost any prayer or meditation skill where going to a higher level is important: 1. to feel one with the Universe, or 2. to talk to God, 3. to view life's problems from a higher plane or a Soul perspective, rather than a body/fear level, or 4. to ride the upflow vortexes to your Guides' or Guardian Angels' level rather than their having to come "down" to your frequency. Think of the "Soul you" as a kind of bubble of consciousness that can be uplifted in that upflow energy. By the way, since superstrings, "Soul" is no longer just a religious term to me. Ever since superstrings, I've felt I could talk to an atheist or agnostic and say "you as a Soul" and mean "you and your other six dimensions we don't have the technology to measure yet—your full bubble of consciousness." Upflow vortexes can also stretch your bubble of consciousness and expand it (like filling up a balloon). The upflow helps you expand and blend more easily with the greater Whole. Blending with the clouds, the sky, or the heavens is easier in an upflow vortex. Tapping universal consciousness, or oneness with what the Native Americans call the Great Spirit or what many people refer to as macroconsciousness, is made easier in an upflow vortex.

Inflow Energy

Inflow vortexes are very different. There, energy flows into the planet. That flow pattern turns your reflections inward. Any prayer or meditation where introspection is a key factor will be turbo-boosted in an inflow vortex. The inflow energy helps you to go within more easily. If you want to understand and/or heal something from your past or go inward for past-life memory, those skills will be enhanced in an inflow vortex.

No one type of vortex is better than another. What matters is using the type of vortex that is best suited to the meditation that is of interest to you. It's a tragedy to see people come to Sedona and go to the wrong site for the spiritual skill they want to attain or practice. Trying to work on healing an inner hurt or going in for a past-life memory in an upflow vortex is automatically more difficult. One woman described just such an effect when she went to Bell Rock (an upflow vortex area) to try to clear an old hurt from her past. "I felt great, but I didn't get a damn thing accomplished. Every time I tried to go inward I kept getting a feeling of, Oh, who cares? Just blend with the universe!" Can you blend with the universe in an inflow area? Of course you can. But for the average person whose control is not fully refined, it is like trying to swim upstream in a powerful river. Going against the current tends to stop them dead in the water. As a result, they experience little or nothing—or worse, headaches and frustration from trying so hard to go against the energy flow.

How to Find and Identify Vortexes

Upflow vortexes will tend to be associated with mountains, mesa tops, and pyramidal-type topography. Inflow vortexes will be associated with valleys, canyons and caves. Use the symbology on page 15 to help you remember the topography associated with each form of vortex (Upflow - Mesa or Mountain Peak, Inflow - Valley or Canyon) You can use the geographical characteristics of an area to help you determine what the flow pattern of the area should be, but the bottom line is that you can feel it. In fact, you have in all probability already experienced vortex energy, but were just not aware of it. For instance, I'm sure at some point in your life you have been to a scenic overlook. How would you describe your feeling as you stood looking at the view? Do you remember the strong feeling of expansiveness and stretching that you felt at overlooks? Most overlooks are ei-

19

ther upflow areas or upflow/lateral-flow combination areas. That is why they generate that euphoric feeling of expansion. What is most significant is not that you felt the energy, but rather that you didn't have to be the world's greatest psychic or "om" in your car for twenty minutes before walking to the edge to experience the effect. Now that you know what to look for, you can literally find areas of vortex energy wherever you travel. You can make any trip a vortex retreat. Think of the freedom that ability can give you to create your own enlightenment and quality of life.

What do you think I tell my Manhattan students who need the unwinding effect and harmony of an upflow area in their lives but complain that they are stuck in New York City with no vacation time for the next several months? I tell them to go to the top of the Empire State Building. It's not as good as going to the Catskill Mountains or the Rockies, but skyscrapers have a stronger component of upflow energy than the surrounding street-level environment. As a result, that difference can provide a smaller, but sufficiently strong, turbo-boost to get your perspective or a depression unstuck.

Understanding/Matching Labeling Systems

Now let's start matching terminologies. Remember that Free Soul uses the upflow/inflow labeling system because it more easily helps you identify what spiritual skills will be turbo-boosted by each site. If you have skipped ahead to this page it is imperative that you read pages 12-20 first to fully understand this next section.

Electric/Magnetic

What do most people think about when they think about magnetism? Attraction. A magnet can attract or repel, but our dominant association with magnets is attraction (as with refrigerator magnets). Every place you see labeled a magnetic vortex always is an inflow area. Page Bryant herself, personally told me when she was leaving Sedona, "I'm not a scientist. I just used symbolic words that represented what I was feeling at the sites. Magnetic to me meant attraction into Mother Earth." What is our stereotype for electricity? We have all seen a cartoon of people getting a shock or touching a static-electricity generator and their hair standing on end. Every place labeled an electric vortex always has an upflow energy pattern. With this understanding you can see how electric and magnetic are good symbolic (but not literal) labels.

Masculine/Feminine

Another common labeling system for vortexes is masculine or feminine. It's a stereotype, but in general the feminine principle in all of us is better at introspection, at going inward and dealing with feelings. Every place you see labeled a feminine vortex always has an inflow pattern. The masculine principle matches with that outward, assertive expansiveness of the upflow energy pattern. Every place labeled a masculine vortex always has an upflow energy. It is also a stereotype, but to remember the Upflow/Masculine connection think about what gender most wants to climb

Mount Everest, "because it is there!" On a humorous note, when discussing the masculine/feminine labeling system, I always get a mental picture of people out at the sites asking, "How do you tell on these things? Mildred, lift up that rock and see if it's a male or female vortex."

Positive/Negative

Some of the misconceptions about this third labeling system are not as humorous. Many people refer to vortexes as positive or negative vortexes. Most people use these terms in a yin/yang sense (as neither good nor bad, but rather just opposite polarities), but some actually feel there are negative, meaning "bad," sites or evil vortexes. That is not true, but here is how that thought came to be: Upflow vortexes became labeled positive areas because they feel so exhilarating. The energy is expansive, taking you up to higher levels and blending you with a greater Whole. They make you feel incredibly positive. This should give you an understanding into why many seekers want to go to Tibet and the Andes. They are some of the strongest upflow locations on the planet. You feel so euphoric there that you don't care about the harsh climate and the lack of modern facilities and conveniences.

The feeling in inflow vortexes contrasts sharply with an upflow area. An upflow vortex is exhilarating, whereas an inflow area has a more pensive feel to it. Because it is coming down on top of you rather than buoying you up, the energy at an inflow site feels heavier. Further, if people aren't used to introspecting, they do not realize that when you go inward the first things you bump into are your fears, doubts, and uncertainties. As a result, these areas, if not understood and prepared for, can cause people to feel heavy, fearful, and doubtful. Consequently, to some, these areas came to be thought of as negative or even evil.

Let me give you an example of the extent to which this association is ingrained in our subconscious. I'm sure he wasn't consciously aware of it, but George Lucas actually wrote an inflow vortex into the Star Wars Episode V movie, *The Empire Strikes Back*. At one point Yoda says to Luke, "Into that cave you must go. Very strong in the dark side of the Force is it. Find yourself in there will you." Luke goes in and has to confront his inner hatreds and the fact that he has some of the same qualities as Darth Vader. It is very clear that the movie didn't have Yoda take Luke to a mountaintop and say, "Luke, this mountaintop is very strong in the dark side of the Force." Generally our associations with mountaintops are positive and expansive. To illustrate the point further, there are some strong but small inflow areas in Sedona—sinkholes that were named Devil's Kitchen and Devil's Dining Room because people went into them and, compared to the exhilaration of the mesa tops, they felt this heaviness and their doubts and conflicts. Actually, these areas are not good meditation sites, not because they are evil but because they do not have a graded energy pattern. The flow is basically neutral around them except right at the edge or in the sinkhole itself. This can make these locations perilous when people get too close to the edge (and potentially fall) or climb into the sinkhole, creating erosion and environmental damage.

Preventing Negative Meditations

There is also a brain science explanation for why inflow areas can be thought of as negative. When most people go inward for introspective prayer or meditation, they tend to bump into the layer of the brain called the limbic system. This part of the brain is so powerful, brain scientists call it, "the Limbic Brain." It is literally a brain within the brain. It generates over 90% of your negative emotions: your worries, hurts, angers, and fears. Why do we have it? In our evolutionary past the limbic brain helped keep us alive as a species. We were more surviveable miserable than blissed out. If you went walking through the meadow thinking, "Om, isn't life great," something would make you lunch. Either that or you wouldn't gather enough food to survive the winter.

What has occurred is that our technology has advanced faster than our physiology can adapt. In the 1800s you might live your whole life and never see a stagecoach crash or even hear about one. Now, if you live in a major metropolitan area and commute to work, you hear about countless accidents as you listen to the radio or television for traffic patterns, even if you don't see one that day. That affects your limbic brain. The global media makes it worse. We daily hear about some disaster somewhere around the globe, even if all is well in our part of the world. If you don't know how to counter the limbic brain as you meditate on a hurt, worry or anger, you will just get stuck in a "broken record" limbic loop; reexperiencing the worry, hurt, or anger, rather than getting resolution. For the purposes of this book, the Soul-shift technique contained on the upcoming pages can help you counter the limbic brain. When you Soul-shift before going inward, you tend to go in with "wise eyes" with a Soul perspective and not get stuck in limbic. (For more extensive information on methods for eliminating worries, hurts, angers, fears, and countering the limbic brain, for living your life "as a Soul" see my book, *Access Your Brain's Joy Center.*)

How to Quantum-Leap and Tap Vortex Energy More Easily

To fully tap vortex energy it is essential to understand how to reach into those *"six other dimensions we don't have the technology to measure yet."* Knowing how to extend your consciousness into that beyond is the prerequisite skill for receiving the maximum benefit at vortexes. Twenty years of field research and testing has gone into the development of the technique (contained in this section) to make that mental quantum leap easily attainable for you.

The main reason I left the laboratory brain-science environment was because science couldn't explain consciousness to my satisfaction. By the way, consciousness is another area science *still* doesn't have a clue how to measure. Science as yet has been unable to explain how the wiring of the brain creates consciousness. Consciousness is defined as how you recognize you as you and how you create new thought. According to orthodox brain science, you never have a new, independently initiated thought. Orthodox brain science considers every thought you have nothing more than a reaction to sensory stimuli. In fact, there's a story in my book *You Are Psychic!* called "The Day Brain Science Wasn't Enough" that describes the time I literally cornered one of the head professors in the brain-science department at M.I.T. during my senior-year one-on-one tutorial with him. I said, "Professor, I took your course and learned that if we stimulate a particular cell in the motor strip it will cause the leg to move. Also, when the leg is moved we can see that cell firing. Everyone in the class went, `Ahhh, now I understand.' But I still *don't* understand. What makes that cell fire when we want to *initiate* movement?"

He said, "Actually, what makes that cell fire is some other cell deeper in the brain." We spent ten minutes tracing nerve pathways in the brain, and I finally asked, "What's the bottom line? Where does the process start?" He got somewhat embarrassed and responded, "Well, I guess it would have to be some cell in the retina or in the auditory mechanisms." I said, "You're describing a robot, something that merely reacts to the world around it. Don't you feel like you create new thought?" "Yes, I do," was his response "How does science explain that?" I asked. "We can't," was his embarassed reply.

That was in 1971. If you've watched the PBS series on the brain, you know that science still doesn't have a clue how to explain consciousness based on the wiring of the brain. Personally, I feel it is probably another of the areas that extends into those "six other dimensions we don't have the technology to measure yet." As a result, I decided to leave the academic environment and look in the laboratory of life for the answer to this question. In my world travels I tried to learn more about tapping the Soul, the source of consciousness. My strongest ability psychically is aura vision. Everywhere I traveled I looked at people's auras. What does the aura of a monk in meditation look like? How is the aura of a Swiss watchmaker different? From thousands of observations and from field tests with students worldwide I developed the concepts and approaches that led to this technique.

Locating the Soul's Extradimensional Energy

It's absurd to try to describe in three-dimensional terms the location of the ten-dimensional bubble of consciousness that you are as Soul energy. It's even more ridiculous to try to draw it on a two-dimensional sheet of paper. The best approximation is to say that most of the energy that you are as a Soul actually exists outside of the body, above and slightly behind the head area (see Figure 2). That is why most people see an aura for the first time above the head of an individual. If an aura were simply a biomagnetic effect, you'd actually have stronger energy fields just above the ears (this is the level of the corpus callosum, the huge bundle of neurons that connects the right and left brain) or in the solar plexus (abdominal area) where all the ganglia are. Nine out of ten people see their first aura above the head of another individual. They are seeing that person's Soul-energy field rather than the body-energy field. This also explains why paintings of saints and religious figures always show the halo as predominantly above the head. Even if they don't see auras, people sense a radiance, a presence, there.

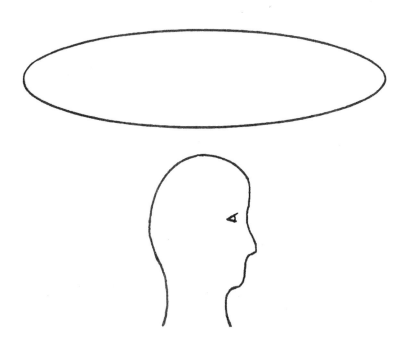

Figure 2. Soul-energy field relationship to the body

A good way to think of that Soul-energy field's relation to the body is to think of an upside-down iceberg. As you know, most of an iceberg is below the water with only a small part above. Turn it upside down, and you have a good visual analogy of the relationship of that Soul bubble to the body. Most of the energy of consciousness—that massive, underwater part of the iceberg—is actually above the head area. The small part of the iceberg above the water is like that part of the Soul energy that comes into the body, hooks up with the wiring, and helps us run the machine (see Figure 3).

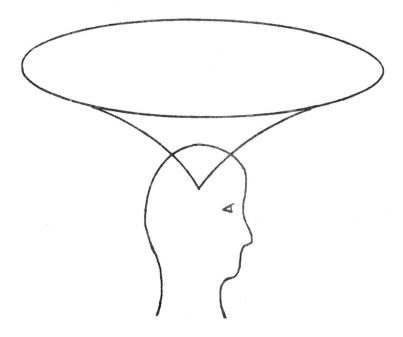

Figure 3. Soul energy connection into the body

Most of our life we've been trained to focus our awareness down and out the physical senses (Figure 4). That process is essential if you are to effectively function in a three-dimensional universe.

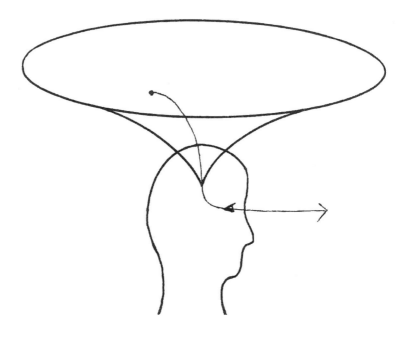

Figure 4. Awareness out thru the physical senses

In Free Soul we have developed a technique called the Soul-shift that teaches you how to turn that focus back inward and up to those deeper dimensions (Figure 5). Every form of meditation eventually gets you there. The problem is that most of them take too long—ten, twenty or thirty minutes. The best spiritual technique or meditation is effectively worthless in daily life if it takes too long, because you won't use it in your normal routine when you may need it the most. Everything that I have developed and taught through Free

30

Soul is designed to work in minutes. This *"Inner Technology"®* makes the spiritual skills of the mountaintop accessible to you in the real-world village of life.

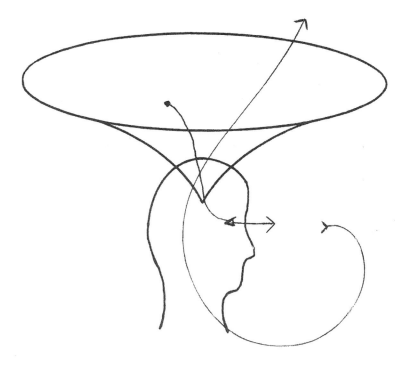

Figure 5. Focusing in and up to Soul dimensions

The mechanics are very simple: You just start to become more aware of your own body than your environment, and then you focus that awareness in your lower legs—your feet, your ankles, your calves. Gradually, you shift that focus up through your body, like riding upward on an elevator of awareness. When you get to the head area you just make one

31

more focus shift. Most people experience this final shift as taking a step into a vaster space. If in trying to make that final shift, you feel pressure in the forehead and eye area, you are trying to turn your eyeballs back and take them out there with you. Leave them where they belong! Do the shift more as a feeling of sensing that space above the head.

Avoid the Overtrying Trap

Also, *do not* try, force, or concentrate. Whenever you overtry, you cut off your experience and throw yourself into the voluntary nervous system (which controls your muscles and the *physical* senses). The involuntary nervous system is what interfaces with all psychic, spiritual, biofeedback, and mind/body healing skills. Understanding this is crucial to easily accessing your deeper dimensions.

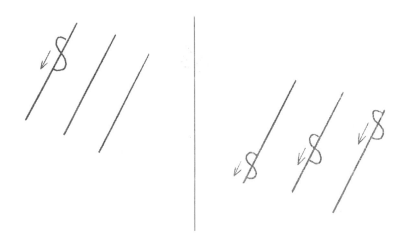

Figure 6. The voluntary nervous system

Each of us actually has two separate nervous systems within our bodies. The voluntary nervous system (that runs your muscles and physical senses) is basically a series of dormant wires (see Figure 6). When you think about moving an arm or leg, you activate a group of nerve fibers. The more you concentrate, the more fibers you activate and the result is that you get more individual muscle-bundle control (and thus better performance). The involuntary nervous system is different from its voluntary cousin in that it is always active (instead of staying dormant until you need it). The involuntary nervous system is constantly functioning to maintain your homeostatic balances (your temperature, blood pressure, pH balance, etc.). The secret to influencing the involuntary system (the control that contains the psychic/spiritual interface) is to nudge it into making different loops and following little-used pathways (Figure 7).

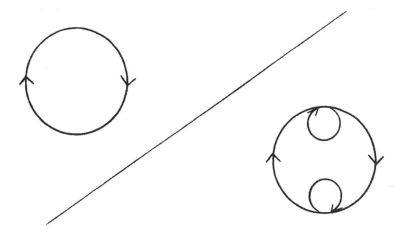

Figure 7. The involuntary nervous system

33

The minute you try too hard or overconcentrate, you merely activate your voluntary nervous system. The result is increased muscle tightness and physical-sense dominance—and thus a reduction in your spiritual attunement. Throughout most of our life the skills we have learned (walking, talking, reading, writing, driving, etc.) have been physical-sense dominant and controlled by the voluntary nervous system. Now it is time to learn a new form of thinking, *focused* rather than *forced* awareness, to learn how to attend without having to try or overconcentrate. To maximize your experience in the vortexes you need to have an attitude of allowing, while you explore, focus and guide your awareness, rather than forcing. If you force, you will interface primarily with your voluntary nervous system, and your physical senses will dominate rather than your psychic ones.

Soul-Shift Warm-Up Exercises

The best physical analogy I can give you of the feel of focusing rather than forcing is the difference between staring and peripheral vision. If you stare at something you will notice that you experience a feeling of concentration, a sense of forcing. If instead you try to notice something off to the side in your peripheral vision, you can't force that. You have to allow it to come to you. That "allowing" openness is the form of focus you want to use for tapping deeper dimensional effects to the maximum.

Here is another way to experience how to attend without forcing. (Have a partner help you with this if somebody is available). Put a hand about 18 inches in front of your eyes. Notice how your awareness of the hand keeps you physically focused. Now instead, put a hand above the head, up in that Soul area. Try to sense where the hand is. Can you feel how when you sense where the hand is, your attention is pulled upward? Notice how you can attend there without having to force.

Tapping the Extradimensionality of the Soul

The process outlined below will guide you in making that upward shift and exploring the fullness of your extradimensional Soul energy. The effect is like a slingshot, propelling you up and out to your own deeper consciousness. You will feel boundaries dissolve as you step into this more expansive part of your being. You will feel the peace and heightened awareness available to you there. Do not try to analyze what you are sensing during the technique. That will only create tension and cut off or limit your experience. Review your impressions later.

Making the Soul-Shift

1. Relax, sit comfortably, and close your eyes.

2. Gradually increase awareness of yourself rather than of your environment. Do not try or concentrate, but gently focus your awareness on what you are feeling from and within yourself.

3. Next, pay specific attention to your lower legs. Feel your feet, your ankles, your calves. Slowly begin to shift your focus up through your legs, hips, waist, chest, and shoulders, etc. As you sense each body area and are moving upward, gradually leave behind the parts you have already sensed. Tune them out. Ride this mental elevator upward until you reach the head area.

4. As you focus on the head, take time to feel all the thoughts and memories that are you. Briefly let yourself see what comes to mind when you focus on yourself as a person.

5. Shift your focus one more level upward to the Soul area. Some people experience this final focus shift as a feeling of stepping out of the top of their heads into a vaster space. Notice how the boundaries seem to disappear and you feel as if you are in an expanding dimension. Feel your awareness of yourself deepen, as if you have stumbled onto a seldom-explored but richer part of yourself. You may even feel you can extend outward limitlessly in any direction. This is the Real You. You have become aware of your Soul nature.

- Remember: If you feel any pressure in your forehead or eye area as you make this final focus shift, you are probably trying to turn your eyes backward and force them to look out of the back of your head. They will not go there, so leave them where they belong. Make that final focus shift more a feeling of letting your mind float, or a heightened awareness of the space above you.

6. Explore this deeper part of yourself. See how far you can stretch. See if you can touch into the corners of the room or even beyond the room.

7. Then let something distract you (a sound or a physical awareness) and do a touch-and-go. Come back to the body, bounce, and go right back up to that Soul area.

8. On this trip sense the timelessness you feel in this extradimensional state. Experience the peacefulness that radiates through you as you tap the extensiveness of your full consciousness.

9. When you are finished, gently shift your focus back down to the head area and note some specific part of your body (nose, mouth, hands, etc.). Slowly move a finger or foot, and when you feel ready, open your eyes. Gently move your body to restore your normal physical orientation.

This technique is only the first step on a long and fascinating journey into the extra dimensions of the Soul. The more you meditate and practice the process, the easier it will be to tune out distractions. The more you experience your Soul, the easier it will be to make that final up-and-out focus shift. Exploring your extra dimensions can also be a natural relaxer. Tapping the Soul even briefly relieves the pressure of the physical world. In most instances one's aura will unwind and expand two to six inches by the time the exercise is completed. Once you learn control, the Soul-shift can be used at will throughout your day.

37

How to Maximize Your Vortex Meditations

For meditation the Soul-shift technique is literally like a spiritual Hubble telescope. The space-based telescope is infinitely superior to land-based observatories because it is above the distorting effects of the atmosphere. When you make the Soul-shift, not only does your alpha brain-wave pattern markedly increase, you also rise above the static of the three-dimensional realm. That deeper, less distorted perspective makes any meditation exercise easier, stronger, and faster. In a vortex area, if you Soul-shift first as an attunement preliminary, your experience will be clearer and more profound. Consciously making the Soul-shift is not as crucial in an upflow vortex. Upflow areas tend to automatically shift people. That is one of the reasons upflow vortexes feel so exhilarating. In upflow areas the touch-and-go concept is the most important technique to prevent the memory-wiping effect of blissing out.

How to Prevent Blissing Out

As you do the Soul-shift technique bring yourself back at one point and practice doing a touch-and-go as a preventative to blissing out. "Touch and go" is an aviation term. Pilots practice coming into a landing strip, but instead of landing, they touch down with their wheels and then take off again. Spiritually, the touch-and-go concept is the way to prevent blissing out (refer to page 42). You can come back and touch base with the earth and your body whenever you feel you're losing control.

38

The Effectiveness of the Working Meditation

The key to the touch-and-go process is to go as deeply as you can without losing control and spacing out. Next, capture one impression (feeling, image, thought, or phrase), come back to the body and write it down (even if you don't understand its meaning at the moment). Then bounce and go right back out to that deeply blended state. Continue this process in cycles, retrieving a piece, coming back to record your impressions, bouncing, and going out again. This is what in Free Soul we call a working meditation. Not only does this give you greater control of your meditative process, but you can actually bring through more information than you ever thought possible and in half the time. Each time you come back you are taking a pebble out of the dam. With every touch-and-go—record and return—you open a wider channel for more information to flow through.

The Importance of Recording Your Impressions

You should always bring a pen and paper or a recording device with you on your vortex meditations. If you don't, when you get an insight your first reaction is, "I hope I don't forget that!" As a minimum, that worry cuts off the flow and slams shut your mental hatch to the deeper dimensions. Frequently the mental static created by worrying about remembering will also cause you to forget your impressions more easily. When you know how to do the touch-and-go, you simply make a quick note and bounce back for more. If you utilize this process you will be amazed at how quickly your meditations can be completed and the depth of solutions that you can easily self-channel.

Travel Inward with a Soul Perspective

In inflow vortexes making the Soul-shift first is crucial. Without the Soul-shift people tend to go inward to the limbic brain and get stuck in a critical state of mind, judging themselves (with inner talk like, "How could I have done that?" or "Why was I so stupid?"). When you Soul-shift first, you travel inward with a loving, Soul, perspective, seeking learning not blame. Positive affirmations or meaningful religious prayers before meditation can have a similar effect. It is important to realize, however, that some worries, hurts, angers, or fears are so powerful that no matter what you do, you can find yourself stuck in that limbic loop. If that happens the secret is to get up and walk your meditation. Sitting is the worst posture for meditating or praying on problems. You will tend to sit and stew, getting stuck in limbic. The brain scientists say that anything that pulls you out to higher cortex, can break that limbic lock. To walk, you have to use parts of the motor strip (in the higher cortex) to run the muscles of your legs. That is why people can often sit at the beach and stay depressed. When they walk the beach, they inevitably feel better. That is also the reason people are building labyrinths (walking meditation paths). If you must sit, use a rocking chair or journal (record your impressions as you meditate). To write you have to use motor strip areas for the muscles in the hand, as well as language centers in the higher cortex of the brain.

Enhancing Communication with Your Guides

Making the Soul-shift first will also improve your communication with your Spirit Guides (Guardian Angels). It puts you closer to their frequency. You have less static from the three-dimensional realm to distract you from what they are trying to communicate to you. Free Soul also has a private counseling session in which we teach a method for achieving direct communication with your Guides that is independent of the psychic senses. This technique makes it possible for you to get answers from your Guides even when you are psychically closed off (due to pressures or circumstances). It also provides a method to double check what you are getting psychically in your meditations. This way you can be sure you are interpreting both the source (whether it is from your Guides, your Higher Self, or just other people's or other entities' random or deliberately pressuring thoughts) and the interpretation (what the symbol means, if the message is for now or later in the year, etc.) of the impressions you are receiving. This Guidance-Communication Technique is shown as part of Free Soul's Introductory Soul Profile (FS001 Counseling). The session also includes an analysis of what your psychic strengths are and extensive information about the spiritual energies that are currently affecting your life.

To find out about Counselors available in Sedona or in locations around the country, contact the Free Soul National Office at P.O. Box 1762, Sedona, AZ 86339 or look on our web site - http://freesoul.net

Finding the Right Spot at a Vortex

One of the reasons that Bell Rock is such a good meditation site is that it has a nicely graded energy pattern. Lower down, the upflow energy is more gentle. As you progress higher up the upflow becomes more laserlike (see Figure 8).

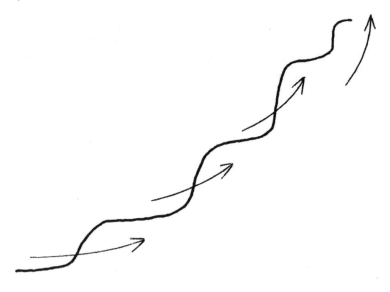

Figure 8. Bell Rock's graded energy pattern

Keep in mind that higher is not necessarily better. One of the drawbacks of upflow vortexes is that they can cause you to "bliss out." That is not a problem if that is what you are going to the upflow vortex for. Upflow vortexes are the best spiritual stress-reduction sites. They literally unwind you and help you tap that universal oneness and harmony. When you are going to the upflow area for a specific

42

meditation (to view a problem from a Soul level or to commune with your Guides), however, blissing out seems to wipe the memory tape. You feel great, but you can't remember what you received in the meditation. Remember earlier in this booklet I described the "Touch and Go" technique for preventing this bliss-out memory-loss effect (see page 38). Many people ask, "What is the best spot on Bell Rock to meditate?" Once again, the answer is, "Yes." Find the place that feels right to you. You have to honor and trust your inner sense. What you're looking for is the location that has the right amount of uplift to turbo-boost you without having to fight for control to keep from blissing out. In years past I actually had my young sons, Brian and Michael, almost all the way up Bell Rock meditating with me. Most of the time when I go on my own, however, I only go to the first or second level. I pick the location that has the intensity of energy flow that matches my needs. That spot will not only vary from person to person, but also from day to day. The same is true for inflow areas. Trust your feelings as you look for the spot to meditate. Let your intuition guide you to the area that has just the right amount of inflow to take you inward gently (and under control).

Vortexes and Native American Spiritual Practices

Native Americans have always used vortex areas for their sacred practices. Depending on which type they used, they developed different spiritual practices. Most of the northern Indians would use upflow vortexes. Through fasting, exhaustion—or in the extreme, being bitten by a rattlesnake—an altered state would be attained. Then they would go into an upflow vortex (a mesa top or a mountaintop) and go upward to receive their vision from the Great Spirit. The southern Indian tribes had a stronger spiritual focus on going inward to meet and confront their inner demons. The writings of Carlos Castaneda on the teachings of Don Juan illustrate this process. Usually valleys, canyons, and caves would be used for that inner journey.

Vortexes and Healing

Many people ask, "What vortex is best for healing?" The answer is, "Yes." It depends on the type of healing skill you wish to utilize. Many people with a strong Native American heritage prefer a form of healing that entails grounding with Mother Earth. An inflow vortex will best turbo-boost that approach. An inflow vortex is also best for a healing method that pulls energy from the universe. Personally, I prefer to practice a form of self-healing that utilizes an upflow vortex. First, I let the upflow energy polish my aura and carry the debris out of it. I also use the upflow effect to draw strength and energy from the rock. This "rock recharging" is not just mumbo jumbo; it's actually based on Einstein's equation $E = mc^2$. Before that equation science used to think that energy and matter were completely separate entities.

$E = mc^2$ basically means that matter is just another form of energy. In the same way that we have steam, water and ice, we have spiritual energy, physical energy (like light and heat), and matter. Matter is nothing more than the ice form of energy. It's hypercondensed energy. You experience an analogous tapping of stored energy every time you use a battery or operate electronic items like computers (that use capacitors to store energy). Matter is nothing more than highly condensed stored energy. That's why a nuclear weapon makes such a huge explosion: It releases the tremendous amount of energy that is stored in a very small amount of matter. Because the Soul is one of the most refined of energies, it can harmonize and blend with all other energy forms, including matter. When you learn to Soul-blend, you can literally sink into the rock, blend across the matter boundary, and draw energy from the rock. In the turbo-boost of an upflow vortex you can let that energy flow upward and bring the strength of the rock to you. You can guide the flow to help heal or strengthen a specific area, or you can simply recharge your spiritual batteries and enhance your vitality level.

(Note: Soul-blending is just one of the over 80 spiritual skills taught in Free Soul's 10-Lesson *"Dynamics of Being a Free Soul"* Comprehensive Course available on cassette tape, as a 200 plus page textbook, or from a certified instructor.)

The Significance of the Red Rock

The rock at Sedona's vortex sites is red in color due to a higher than average iron content. The presence of this

45

metal along with the others (such as manganese) makes the rock even more effective as a site for recharging. Metals have a much higher atomic weight and density than silicon (the element that predominantly comprises rock). The result is that metalized rock is literally a turbo-charged form of condensed energy. The red/orange hue of Sedona's rocks is also one of the most neurologically stimulating of colors. Thus physical exhilaration is added to your spiritual efforts. Spiritually, red has always been associated with the most powerful energizing and recharging effects. That enhancing effect and that you can find almost every type of vortex within a small geographic radius, are what makes Sedona special.

Tapping Sedona's Main Upflow Vortexes (Bell Rock and Airport Mesa)

Bell Rock and the Airport Mesa Vortex (see Directions Appendix) are Sedona's main accessible upflow areas. In summer it is wisest to visit them in the early morning because of the heat. The combination of the upflow and strong sun can overwhelm people in the middle part of the day. In the winter midday is the best visitation time because then the added warmth is helpful. If the rock is still cold, it can pull heat from your body as you meditate, causing a hypothermal effect that intrudes on your reflections.

Bell Rock

The graded energy that makes Bell Rock such an effective upflow area has already been explained (see page 42). Its value as a meditation site is also enhanced by the ease with which the average hiker can get to the various levels. Never underestimate, however, the potential danger of climbing on the loose rock surfaces (especially in wet weather). In upflow areas it is always wise to decide conservatively whether you should sit or climb to a particular area. The upflow makes you feel like you can soar. That feeling, if not balanced, can override common sense. Further, while the upflow does assist your upward climbing efforts, it works against you when coming down (when most falls occur).

Remember also that higher is not necessarily better. Going too high may merely space you out and prevent effective meditation. All these warnings notwithstanding, Bell Rock is a definite must on any vortex meditation agenda. It was on Bell Rock that I made my decision to found Free Soul in Sedona.

Many people complain about the lack of complete quiet on Bell Rock (because sound travels upward, you can clearly hear the passing traffic). To me that road noise is a plus. It forces you to practice self-channeling in a more realistic environment. If you learn to tune in only when you are in complete silence, the breakthroughs and skills you experience will not be as accessible in your daily life.

Airport Mesa

The main Airport Mesa Vortex (the small hill to the left of the larger flat mesa) is the only place in Sedona where you can get a 360-degree panorama of the entire Sedona/Oak Creek Canyon area. If you are visually oriented, meditating on Airport Mesa can help you capture the feeling of being in the world but not of it. You can see the city and thus be aware of humanity, but you also feel connected to the heavens and beyond. Look for the trail that winds around to the left at the base of the small hill. It provides an easier and safer access to the summit than climbing up the rock faces.

Soul-Projecting from Chapel of the Holy Cross

Actually, Courthouse Butte (seen above), the massive, monlithic slab to the east of Bell Rock, is Sedona's most powerful upflow area. Unless you have a helicopter, however, you can't get on top of it. That is one of the reasons the Chapel of the Holy Cross is included in the Directions Appendix. From the chapel you can see in one glance three of Sedona's strongest areas, Cathedral Rock, Bell Rock, and Courthouse Butte. Once you know how to do the Soul-shift, you don't have to be physically in the vortexes to tap their energy. When you know how to Soul-shift (pages 25-37), you can shift up and Soul-project to the sites. From the Chapel of the Holy Cross you can easily tap both the upflow of Courthouse Butte and Bell Rock and the combination vortex energy (to be discussed later) of Cathedral Rock. There is a trail that runs between the base of Bell Rock and the base of Courthouse Butte. Many people find this generally level walk inspirational and feel that they get a sufficient amount of upflow from viewing the rocks as they stroll.

Aside from the skills described earlier (see pages 17-18) that vortexes can turbo-boost, upflow vortexes are also the best areas for sending a prayer or affirmation out to the universe or to the future. They are not, however, the best locations for future sensing. If you try to sense the future in an upflow area, usually all possible futures become blurred together. The *best* locations for future scanning are lateral-flow areas.

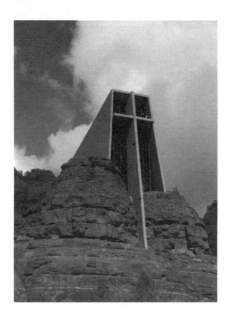

Riding the Waves of Time

(in Lateral-Vortex Areas)

Science, language, and our subconscious associations all tend to picture time as lateral. We use expressions such as "the river of time" or "the time tape." In physics and cosmology classes Figure 9 is frequently used to illustrate our relationship to possible futures. Think of the cube as a symbol for our three-dimensional universe flowing along the river of time. In front of us are spread many possible futures.

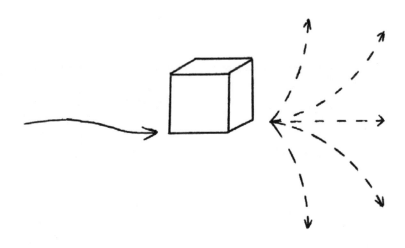

Figure 9. The river of time and futures scanning

In a lateral-flow area it seems to be easier for people to Soul-blend (one of the many skills taught in the *Dynamics of Being a Free Soul* Comprehensive Course) into the dimension of time. In a lateral-flow area you can more easily scan the possible futures that spread out in front of you. You can picture different options (move to city A, move to city B, or take job A or job B, etc.) as being at different angles in front of you. When you know how to Soul-shift (pages 25-37), you can shift up and Soul-project into the various options and feel them. Some options will feel solid and positive. Others will feel shaky, evanescent, or negative.

Scanning the future is always fuzzy, because the future is not formed yet. Lateral-flow vortex areas and this technique make it possible to scan across possible futures in a clearer, more controlled manner. Almost all overlooks have a strong lateral-flow component. In the Sedona area the best one is at the Oak Creek Canyon Overlook (17 miles north of Sedona on Hwy 89A at the top of the switchbacks on the road to Flagstaff: see Directions Appendix).

Tapping Sedona's Inflow Energy (and Red Rock Crossing)

Most of Sedona (excluding the cliffs and mesas, of course) is a huge inflow area. Sedona itself lies in the bowl of a valley cut by Oak Creek. You can effectively tap some of the inflow energy almost anywhere, but the best location for inflow meditation is at Red Rock Crossing for two reasons. First, as you drive down to Red Rock Crossing (see Directions Appendix) you will feel as though you are descending into the heart of Sedona. It even looks that way. The second benefit of the Red Rock Crossing location is the water of Oak Creek. Frequently when you go inward you touch issues and feelings from the past that hurt or can cause regret. The flow of water seems to help soothe those hurts and release the old patterns. The water also assists in cleansing your aura and nurturing new beginnings. Also, don't discount the sound. The babbling brook sound helps to pull you out of limbic. That is why many people are putting faux waterfalls in their homes and/or backyards. All three of these effects are helpful when doing introspective meditations (remember the importance of Soul-shifting before going inward).

Inward meditation can go even beyond this lifetime into the exploration and clearing of past-life Soul bruises. These are unresolved conflicts from a previous life that, like scar tissue, can negatively impact on this life's happiness. The lateral-flow aspect of Oak Creek also makes Red Rock Crossing an ideal location for doing past-life memory work. You can combine the inward reflection with blending into the water and symbolically traveling upstream—back in time—into your pasts. It is also possible to tap into a sense of the eons of lifetimes you have already experienced. Through the water you can flow into the timelessness of the Soul.

The best location for this type of meditation is upstream from the Red Rock Crossing parking area. Take the level path 1/4 mile past the tall trees to the red rock beach area (no sand, just level red rock). There the water is only six inches to a foot deep. In the summer you can even sit comfortably in the creek or dip your feet in the cool waters to do your meditation. Take care when walking on the creek bottom, however, because the flat rock can at times be slippery. In winter sitting by the water at the beach area can be as effective as being in the water itself.

At various times through the year (spring in particular) Oak Creek is in flood and the red rock beach area is completely underwater and unusable as a meditation site. At these times it is strongly recommended to sit on the banks for meditation, staying out of the water. The flood currents are much more powerful than they appear.

The Specialness of Combination Vortexes

You will remember that in the early nomenclature three types of vortexes were described: electric, magnetic, and electromagnetic vortexes. As stated earlier, not only are these labels scientifically inaccurate, but the term electromagnetic is even more misleading, because *all* of life is electromagnetic. In Free Soul we refer to the areas previously called electromagnetic vortexes as "combination areas" because they have a combination of both inflow and upflow energy.

These places *are* special because the combination of the two flow patterns in one location turbo-boosts advanced, more complex, spiritual skills and meditations. The combined inflow and upflow energy helps you integrate the multiple perspectives and skills needed for dealing with life's complexities.

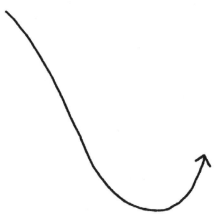

Figure 10 Mini-upflow in a more massive inflow

In Sedona most of the combination vortexes have the energy pattern shown in Figure 10, a mini-upflow in the midst of a more massive inflow energy pattern. These areas topographically are usually smaller mesas within a larger valley area.

For Spiritual Problem-Solving

The combination vortexes with the pattern shown in Figure 10 (mini-upflow in the midst of a more massive inflow) are outstanding for spiritual problem-solving. They can help you self-channel breakthrough spiritual insights for solving even the most mundane earthly problems.

The strong inflow helps you remember that you came to planet Earth for a reason. To me there are only two choices: Either you feel you were a Soul just floating around and got too close to people having sex—and oops! stuck in a body again—or you believe that you came here to experience the complexities of this three-dimensional realm. By the way, in the terminology of *upflow* and *inflow*, what do you think the dominant energy pattern of planet Earth is, with its gravity? That's right, inflow! Does that give you a clue why life is frequently so difficult? You hear people say things like "Life is hell on Earth!" or "Purgatory is here!" Life *is* challenging. Compared to being a free-floating Soul, being stuffed into a body that has to be fed, clothed, and sheltered creates complexities. Complexities is a euphemism for problems. Everybody has problems. The secret is to not let the scenery of the problems dominate your attention; to prevent the worry from affecting your state of mind, your happiness.

In the mini-upflow of Sedona's combination areas you can soar back up and remember that your spiritual heritage is to *Be a Soul* that *has* a body! And that the problems are just the scenery to help you learn from the play of life. If you have a particular difficulty that is distressing you, hold it in mind as you start your meditation in the combination-vortex area. Then ask, "What is a Soul approach for handling this?" or "How would my Guides or Angels handle this if they had a body?" This will trigger the wisdom of the mountaintop (that higher-level spiritual perspective) and bring it into the village of your daily physical life.

The Reason for Medicine Wheels

Because they are particularly suited to spiritual problem-solving, Sedona's combination vortex areas are places where medicine wheels have historically been built. There are many different traditions and rituals associated with the medicine wheel concept. Here is a simple explanation of one of the many uses of the medicine wheel. Many Native American cultures felt that a rounded perspective where everyone spoke their own truth was more advantageous than a single view, and that problems were frequently the result of too narrow a focus. After building a wheel of sacred stones, the wise elders of the tribe would sit around it. The individual with the problem would come into the center and walk the wheel, stating his/her dilemma. Then each person around the circle would speak in turn. You can capture this same effect even if you are alone at a medicine wheel by picturing your Spirit

Guides sitting around the wheel and sharing their perspective with you one at a time.

You don't even need to build a medicine wheel to tap this self-channeling technique. Building a wheel is actually a disruption to an environment that belongs to everyone (even those who do not value or believe in vortexes). Some tribes also consider it a sacrilege to leave a medicine wheel in place. Those traditions feel that a medicine wheel should be built, used, and then returned to the Earth. In Free Soul we recommend that if people feel the need for a medicine wheel, they make it a mental one. If you feel the need for a physical wheel, then we recommend that you visit those existing on private (but open to the public) land rather than constructing one at a National Forest site.

Boynton Canyon, Nestled within Mother Earth

Because it is narrower, many people feel Boynton Canyon provides a more intimate inward experience. Compared to the vastness of many Sedona sites (which tends to trigger visual people), Boynton Canyon gives many the feeling of being nestled within the arms of Mother Earth. That effect seems to help people higher in Psychic Feeling maximize their combination vortex experience.

The primary Boynton Canyon trail is level. This adds a lateral component that many people use to combine meditation with a sense of walking back in time. To capture the maximum mini-upflow in a more massive inflow combination energy (for spiritual problem-solving) take the secondary trails up to the small mesas that contain the canyon.

There are also some ruins high in the walls of the canyon (that at this writing are still open to the public). These provide a unique eagle's nest-type meditation site. Follow the primary trail along the eastern border of the Enchantment Resort. At the very end of the resort you will see a small trail leading off to the right (east) up the cliffs to the ruins. It is a 10- to 20-minute steep, unprotected climb that is not recommended for people with medical problems or fear of heights.

The ruins as of this writing remain unprotected, so it is imperative that your visit and meditation do not in any way disturb the existing structures or surrounding stones. Also, do not park within the Enchantment Resort, as they will ticket and tow cars of nonguests.

For Positive Past-Life Memory

The one type of vortex you don't find a lot of in the Sedona area is illustrated by Figure 11. This is the pattern that you find in the high valleys of the Rockies or in the valleys of Tibet. It is also found at Crater Lake in Oregon (with the additional benefit of the water energy). The saddle area of Cathedral Rock is the one place in Sedona with this pattern. This mini-inflow in the midst of a more massive upflow is outstanding for retrieving *positive* past-life memory. (As mentioned before, past-life memory is frequently traumatic because when you backscan you generally encounter the glitches in the memory tape, the unresolved issues.)

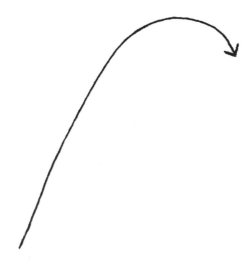

Figure 11. Mini-inflow in a more massive upflow

In the type of combination vortex illustrated in Figure 11 you can use the energy pattern to pull through the memory of past-life masteries. That wisdom can help you with difficulties you face in this life. The strong upflow helps you to go deeply into Soul levels of consciousness. The more gentle inflow then helps you go inward to whatever layer (lifetime) you seek. Just as a pearl is formed one layer at a time, so too the Soul pearl consists of layers of lifetimes. If you hold a problem in mind as you make that inward journey, you will automatically be guided to the lifetime that has the wisdom or experience that could be useful in your now.

Cathedral Rock, Symbol of Sedona

To people worldwide Cathedral Rock has symbolically represented both the beauty and spirituality that is Sedona. The primary location for a combination-vortex meditation on Cathedral Rock is in the saddle area (see Figure 12). Because of its unique structure and location in the heart of Sedona, many people feel that at the saddle they are able to experience both of the combination vortex energies described on pages 55 and 60 (see Figures 10 and 11) and tap both the positive past-life memory and spiritual problem-solving skills described earlier.

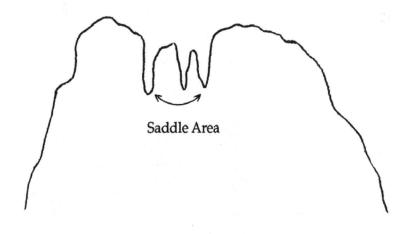

Saddle Area

Figure 12. Combination vortex on Cathedral Rock

The official trial (off Back 'O Beyond Rd.) from the Hwy 179 side of Cathedral Rock is much easier than walking up the paths and washes from Red Rock Crossing (similar in many places to going up stairs two or three steps at a time). Still, however, physically climbing to the saddle is not recommended unless you are a dedicated hiker and in good condition. For most people I again recommend visually tapping the combination vortex energy of Cathedral Rock from either the Chapel of the Holy Cross or sitting at Red Rock Crossing. As mentioned earlier (see page 49), once you know how to Soul-shift, you can Soul-project to the top of Cathedral Rock.

If you do choose to make the actual hike, definitely bring water with you so the effects of dehydration do not interfere with your meditations. It is also recommended that you stay out of washes and gulleys during rain. Flash floods are a possibility and the red rocks can become slippery.

Experience Walking in Love with Life: Explore the West Fork Trail

In our retreats the final location that we recommend to our students is the West Fork Trail in Oak Creek Canyon. Although I consider myself quintessentially practical, I must admit that I think of West Fork as a magical spot. Its biodiversity makes it feel literally alive. Or, to steal a line from George Lucas' *Star Wars* series, it is incredibly strong in the Force. Botanists claim that there are more species of vegetation in the West Fork Trail environment than in any other location in Arizona. That variety, along with the gentle flow of water (of the west fork, of upper Oak Creek) and the canyon walls that rise spectacularly above you, make the West Fork Trail thoroughly magnificent.

Because the energy seems to almost ooze out of the canyon walls, you can practice gathering that force and creating mini-vortexes within your own aura (to turbo-boost yourself later even when you are in the flatlands of Kansas or Florida). The high energy also stimulates the feeling of walking "in love with life." You can also use the lateral flow of West Fork to walk back in time and review your life. Then as you walk out capture the momentum of starting a new life.

If you choose to hike West Fork, wear old shoes, as the trail frequently crosses shallow portions of the creek (on stepping stones). The trail is basically level, but if your balance is imperfect, you may want a walking stick to help as you cross the creek shallows. Also bring food and water, as West Fork is an excellent location for a picnic lunch. Over the years I have seen too many people come out saddened by the fact that they wanted to stay longer but got thirsty or hungry. As with all sites in Sedona, *please pack out your own trash.* When Oak Creek is in flood stage, it is best to pass on hiking the West Fork Trail.

Making Every Day of Your Life a Vortex Retreat

Now that you know this more expanded approach to tapping vortex energy, you can make any trip you take a vortex retreat. Wherever you travel, look for areas of energy flow. Let the topography of the area guide you in what meditations are appropriate to your location. When you are at home, look for local areas around you that have an enhanced upflow or inflow energy compared to the surrounding environment. Use them when you need a turbo-boost for your meditations but are not able or willing to travel. If you utilize the principles outlined in this booklet, you will develop the skills for creating your own enlightenment. You can make life a voyage of discovery into the unlimited potentials that are your birthright as a Free Soul.

Until our paths next cross, whether in person at a Free Soul Retreat or through other Free Soul training materials, know that you are loved and valued for the unique one-of-kind Soul that you are.

Sincerely,

Pete A. Sanders Jr.

<u>Vortex Identification & Directions Appendix</u>
(** = Requires Red Rock Passport)

** BELL ROCK: Strong Upflow

Take Hwy 89A to the "Y" rotary (junction of Hwys 89A and 179) and go south on 179 (to I-17 and Phoenix.) Stay on 179 thru all of Sedona's rotaries toward the Village of Oak Creek. Once you get to the open stretch between Sedona and the Village, look for Bell Rock on your left and signs for Courthouse Vista. Parking Area is on the East side of Hwy 179. If you get to the rotary at Bell Rock Blvd. you have gone too far (you can park at Bell Rock Vista and walk back 1 mile.) Follow trails up the North side of Bell Rock.

** AIRPORT MESA: Upflow

Take Hwy 89A West from the intersection of Hwy 89A and Hwy 179 up the hill. Before the light, turn left onto Airport Rd. (at the circular store building). Go three-quarters of the way up and turn left into the dirt parking area. Follow the designated trail that goes around to the left and up to the top of the middle mesa (equivalent to climbing four flights of stairs).

View from Airport Mesa Vortex

OAK CREEK CANYON OVERLOOK:
Upflow and Lateral Combination

Take Hwy 89A North toward Flagstaff. At the top of the switchbacks (15-17 miles from Sedona) look for the entrance to the overlook on the right. Park and walk out to the vista point (1/4 mile, level).

RED ROCK CROSSING: Strong Inflow (plus Lateral Water-Cleansing Combination)

Take Hwy 89A to the West end of Sedona (toward Cottonwood). At the top of the hill (light after the Sedona Medical Center) make a left on Upper Red Rock Loop Rd. Go down the hill (about 2 miles). At the stop sign at the bottom, turn left and cross a small bridge over a wash. Then turn right and follow signs for the Red Rock Crossing. From the far end of the paid (separate fee area) parking lot walk upstream 1/4 mile (level) to the red rock beach area. Farther upstream are deeper swimming holes.

** SADDLE OF CATHEDRAL ROCK:
Combination Energies

Follow directions to Bell Rock and the Chapel of the Holy Cross. On Hwy 179 go past Chapel Rd. about a mile to Back O'Beyond Rd. (well before you get to Bell Rock). Turn right and take to the end to parking lot on the left. The official trail starts from the back of the lot. The trail is short but VERY Steep in places and not recommended for people with heights anxieties

** BOYNTON CANYON: Combination (Upflow in an Inflow)

Take Hwy 89A West (toward Cottonwood). Just before leaving town turn right on Dry Creek Road. Follow the road three miles to the T. Turn left at the T and follow signs to the Boynton Canyon Trail and Enchantment Resort (a right turn). Park in the trailhead parking lot (before entrance to Enchantment Resort).

CHAPEL OF THE HOLY CROSS AREA:
Combination (& Soul-Projection Site)

Follow the directions for going to Bell Rock. After Radisson Poco Diablo Resort look for signs for the Chapel. Follow the signs and turn left on Chapel Road, which ends at the Chapel parking area. Walk up to the top of the parking area and sit on the rocks there and/or take the spiral ramp (50 yards) to the upper benches.

WEST FORK TRAIL: Energy Wellspring (plus Lateral and Timelessness Effects)

Take Hwy 89A 10-1/2 miles north of Sedona (toward Flagstaff). One and one-half miles past Junipine Resort look for the paid (separate fee area) parking lot on the left (right at the big right-sweeping curve). Walk South along the creek until you come to the bridge over Oak Creek. Once across it turn left and proceed South to the ivy glen and turn right. Walk 1/4 mile until you come to the West Fork of Oak Creek. The mostly level trail starts there. Wear old shoes, as the trail repeatedly takes you through the shallow creek.

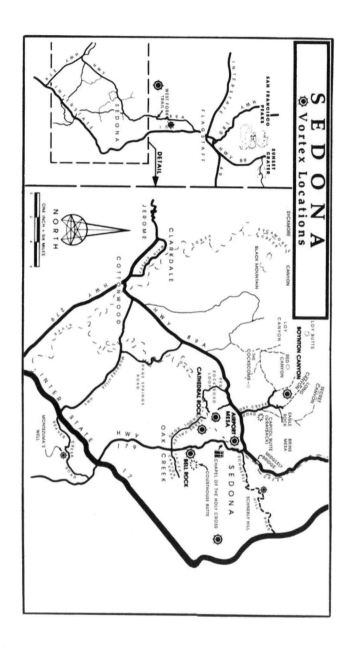

Environmental Awareness and
Sacred Site Etiquette Guide
(Reminders for visiting Archaeological and Vortex Sites
within the Coconino National Forest)

The businesses and residents of Sedona and the rangers of the Coconino National Forest would like visitors to Sedona's vortexes and ruins to remember to help us preserve them for future generations. It is important to treat these environmentally and archaeologically fragile areas with respect and care during your visit. The following simple guidelines to maximize your enjoyment of these areas but still prevent damage to them are recommended.

Please Do!

1. Enter these areas in the spirit of respect for the land, for the great age of the artifacts, and for the significance they hold for many people.

2. Stay on existing trails and obey signs. Where trails are unclear, walk carefully. Much of the native vegetation is very sensitive and does not readily grow back.

3. Be careful; avoid climbing or standing near ledges. The rock here is very soft, is often loose, and may give way easily.

4. Take time for quiet reflection and enjoy the scenic, environmental, and spiritual beauty of these areas. If others are meditating at a site when you arrive, be respectful and keep your voices low.

5. Report it as soon as possible if you see people vandalizing sites or starting fires. The Coconino National Forest Fire & Vandalism Dispatcher's 24-hour line is (928) 526-0600.

Please Don't!

1. Start fires (even candles) of any kind at the sites! The risk of forest fire is real, and even small fires can destroy prehistoric organic materials, ruin the dating potential of artifacts, and damage rock art by covering it with soot.

2. Take home any rocks, rock fragments, or natural vegetation (or cut standing trees or tree limbs). It may seem small to you, but the effect is great if everyone takes home a piece.

3. Pick up or move any rocks or artifacts at a site. If you feel the need to make a medicine wheel at your meditation site, make it a mental one.

4. Draw or scratch graffitti on rocks or cliff faces or touch petroglyphs. Oils from your hands can cause deterioration of the drawings.

5. Camp or sleep in ruins, or dig or remove artifacts in a site. Also, don't add anything (offerings) to a site. This contaminates cultural deposits that are important for scientific tests used by archaeologists in reconstructing past environments and dietary information about the people who occupied these sites.

Additional Notes about Archaeological Sites in the Coconino National Forest. These are the physical remains of a long and diverse occupation of prehistoric, protohistoric, and historic cultures. These remains are a fragile, finite, and nonrenewable resource. The Forest Service is charged with stewardship of these ruins both for public enjoyment and education, and preserving the scientific values of the sites. All archaeological sites in the Coconino National Forest are protected by the Archaeological Resources Protection Act and Federal regulations, which prohibit excavation, removal of any artifacts, damage or alterations, and defacement of archaeological resources on public lands and provides for both felony and misdemeanor prosecution with both imprisonment and fines up to 10 years and $100,000.

How to Reach Free Soul

Contact Free Soul National Headquarters (Sedona) to:

1. Receive information about other self-study materials.
2. Learn about the next National Retreat in Sedona.
3. Dates of Pete Sanders' Programs around U.S..
4. Get phone numbers of Instructors near you
5. Be added to Free Soul's mailing list.

For any or all of the above, write to:

Free Soul
P.O. Box 1762
Sedona, AZ 86339

You can also find us on the internet at:

http://freesoul.net

(See next page for additional training options)

Additional Free Soul Training Options

** Personalized One-on-One Instruction **

Introductory Soul Profile (FS001 Counseling)

A 90 minute Private Session that gives you a wealth of information: how many Spirit Guides you have, which of the psychic Senses is strongest for you, how well your aura is protecting you, and much more. Most important, you will learn how to directly communicate with your Spirit Guides and get answers for the rest of your life.

Accessing Your Brain's Joy Center

A 90 minute Private Session teaching you how to self-trigger the part of the brain that eases limbic stress and counters worries, hurts, angers, and fears. The second step of the Free Soul Triangle for learning to live life, "as a Soul," not stuck in your animal physiological past. (Step one is the Soul-shift contained on pages 25-37)

Soul Infusion

The final leg of the Free Soul Triangle that teaches you how to infuse Soul energy into all facets of your life, for greater Self-Healing skills, enhanced insight and Soul Vision, and deeper harmony in all situations. (Also a 90 min. One-on-One Private Session)

Additional Self-Study Materials

The *Dynamics of Being a Free Soul* Course

A 10-Lesson, 80+ technique integrated course that step-by-step helps you develop your unlimited potentials for mind/body self-healing, Soul awareness, self-understanding, practical psychic sensitivity, and clearing limiting conditioning and programming.

Available as:
1.) a self-study 200+ page textbook
2.) audio version (12 X 90 min. cassettes)
3.) an Instructor-led course (10 X 3-hour lessons)

Sedona Soul and ESP Discoveries Video

Lead in and lead out footage of Sedona with Mr. Sanders teaching in a home setting his introductory Discover *"Inner Technology"*® Workshop. Featured are the scientific explanation of Soul, the Soul-shift, rapid stress reduction, three-perspective psychic scanning, and experiencing the energy of your Spirit Guides.

Free Soul Reflections (Quotations for Journaling)

Available from Local Instructors

The *Dynamics of Being a Free Soul* Course
The Discover *"Inner Technology"*® Workshop
The Access Your Brain's Joy Center Workshop
The Psi 2000 Soul Infusion Workshop
Personalized One-on-One Sessions (listed on page 79)

Orange Cathedral Rock in late afternoon sun
(Photo by John Faulconer of Norfolk, VA)

View of Sedona from Airport Mesa Vortex
(Photo by John Faulconer of Norfolk, VA)

View of Airport Mesa Vortex (middle mounds)
(Photo by John Faulconer of Norfolk, VA)

View of Bell Rock
(Photo by John Faulconer of Norfolk, VA)

View of Couthouse Butte
(Photo by John Faulconer of Norfolk, VA)

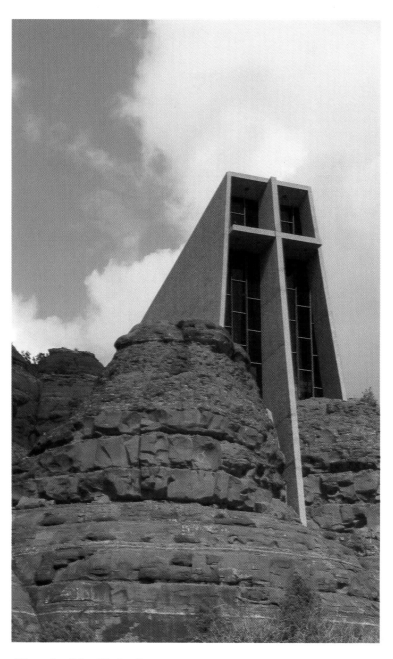

Chapel of the Holy Cross
(Photo by Lori Levin of Sedona, AZ)

View of Submarine Rock
(Photo by John Faulconer of Norfolk, VA)

View of Cathedral Rock (from Red Rock Crossing)
(Photo by John Faulconer of Norfolk, VA)

Cathedral Rock Reflection at Red Rock Crossing
(Photo by John Faulconer of Norfolk, VA)

Cliffs and caves in Boynton Canyon
(Photo by John Faulconer of Norfolk, VA)

Wide view of Boynton Canyon
(Photo by John Faulconer of Norfolk, VA)

Overhanging rock seeps in West Fork Trail
(Photo by John Faulconer of Norfolk, VA)

Fern groves in West Fork Trail
(Photo by John Faulconer of Norfolk, VA)

Inner West Fork Trail cliffs
(Photo by John Faulconer of Norfolk, VA)

Outer West Fork Trail cliffs
(Photo by John Faulconer of Norfolk, VA)

Moon over Cathedral Rock
(Photo by John Faulconer of Norfolk, VA)